Hopeful I Damaged

Poems and Very Short Stories

by

Paul B Morris

nOthing BOOKS

Paul B Morris

Copyright © Paul B Morris 2017

All rights reserved. No part of this book may be reproduced in any form or by any means, except by inclusion of brief quotations in a review, without permission in writing from the author and publisher.

This book is a work of fiction. The characters and situations in this book are as a result of creative imagination and are not real. No resemblance is intended between these characters and any persons living, dead or undead.

This book is sold subject to the condition that it shall not, by way of trade or otherwise, be lent, resold, hired out otherwise circulated without the publisher's prior consent in any form other than that in which it is published.

Published in Great Britain in 2017 by Paul B Morris, Nothing Books Publishing, West Midlands, UK

ISBN-10:1546952462
ISBN-13: 978-1546952466

Photography by Andy Simon
Model Adam Thomas Bane from The Bunker Dungeon
Copyright © Darkslide Photography 2017

Hopeful Dreams and Damaged Nightmares

Thank you to everyone. But, in particular,

Matthew Cash

Amy and Scott Carter @ Southcart Books

Margaret Hammond

Richard Archer

Matt Humphries

Jonathan Butcher

Andy Simon

Becky Brown

Most importantly,

My Children and my family

Helen, my Wife and my Angel!

Hopeful Dreams and Damaged Nightmares

Poetry & Prose

I Wish	8
Image	9
No Words	10
Indicate	11
Listened in the First Place	12
My Son	13
Queen for a Day	14
Like, Like, Like	15
Princess (Leia) in a Box	16
Dark Love	17
Traffic	19
Reflection	20
I am Here	21
Me	22
Chaos	23
Who You Really Are	24
Finally	25

Dark Side Up	26
The Beautiful Game	27
Numb	28
Slave State	30
Headache	31
Black Waters	32
Medication	33
Town Guy	34
Storm	35
Broken	36
Down	37
Crying Clown	38
All my Heart	39
Vitamin D	40
This Life, This Hell	41
Smoke	42
Offend	43
Words are Alive	44

Hopeful Dreams and Damaged Nightmares

The Brutal Reality of Existence	45
16 Years	46
Silent Voice	47
Something True	48
Legs	49
Still A Freak	50
Blood	51
Smile	52
Face	53
Alone	54
Fake	55
Knife	56
This is the Past	57
Chain Reaction	58
Pain	59
Ink	60
Dance	61
Choke	62

In my Arms	63
Mirror Man	64
Tired	65
Four Letter Word	66
When the Medicine Runs Out	67
Torture me Softly	68
Something Else Instead	69
Tears of a Child	70
The Most Wondrous of all Spirits	71
This World for Your Own	72
The Jealousy of Love	73
Prayers	74
Watching Over Us	75
Curses in Verses	76
Angry Man in a Pub	77
Fly	79
A Life Restarted	80
Good Luck	81

Hopeful Dreams and Damaged Nightmares

Picture of You	82
Sprinkles	83
The Man I Used to Be	84
Manufactured Teenage Icon	85
Freedom	86
Wound	87
No Matter	88

A Collection of Very Short Stories

The Pieces Fit	90
Interrogation	94
The Lady with Red Hair in the White Dress	97
Silence	100
This Broken Mind	102
Happy Anniversary	107
Nothing and Something	115
Where Are You?	127

Paul B Morris

Poetry & Prose

A collection of poetry and prose that I have written during 2016 and 2017. Is there any relevance in sharing this particular piece of information with you?

Not really, but you may be like me and interested in statistics. Therefore, this might prove to be an important fact.

Hopeful Dreams and Damaged Nightmares

I Wish

I wish, it was just you and me, following our destiny, living happily ever after.
I wish, that I could be free, why can't I be me, so helpless I'm falling.
I wish, darkness wouldn't call, consuming it all, rendering me worthless.
I wish, my heart wasn't burnt, there's lessons I've learnt, so please let me live now.
I wish, this pain wasn't real, don't know how I feel, how can I end this?
I wish, I accepted my needs, because this cut it bleeds, I need salvation.
I wish, that I could smile, I know it's been a while, so do not forsake me.
I wish, I wasn't a fool, tell me that it's cool, please will you help me.

Paul B Morris

Image

You like to see your face, not that it needs this space.
Your eyes, they lie and distract, I know that it's an act.
Can you take a moment to look at me? Allow yourself, to see what I see.
Associated image placed into your mind, no need to live life in this kind.
A cut so deep, no wonder you weep.

Lose the blade, try to evade.
I see why you cry, you've been sold a lie.
Please can you try, I don't want you to die.
This image reflected, should be rejected.
It's not what I see, you're everything to me.

No Words

There are no words to describe your love.
Only emotions, felt and saved.
Your touch.
And kiss.
A look.
An action so pure.
Forgiveness for some stupid phrase.
Understanding of what is real.
Consideration.
A thoughtful act.
The ability to surprise.
A heart open to sharing a tear.
Your smile.
Eyes wide open and glowing.
Skin so soft.
Dreams shared.
Being safe and secure.
A future and hope.
There are no words to describe my love.
But I'll say it anyway.
I love you.

Indicate

A simple lesson we have to learn
is mirror, signal before you turn.
You failed to do it and in a flash
cars did collide, an horrific crash.
You took a life and sealed a fate
because you failed to indicate.

Listened In The First Place

More angry words and a raging face.
Here we go again.
You say that "if I'd listened in the first place, none of this would have happened".
But, it's not possible to listen to you.
Not for long anyway.
You don't speak to me though and all I hear is noise coming from your direction.
Sounds that aren't completely legible.
Incomprehensible vocabulary that has not point.
Go on, let your fists do the talking.
A language you truly understand.
I'm out of here anyway.
I've no desire to listen.

Paul B Morris

My Son

It is an honour that you're my son,
I am so proud of what you've become.
Despite the challenge in our life,
You've grown so well within the strife.
I've done the best to be your Dad,
Hate the world when you are sad.
But, you have learnt and been so kind,
Respectfully developed your own mind.
Taught all the lessons that I can,
With so much love as my best man.
Admire the way you continue to grow,
You're a person I'm proud to know.
Accepting how I am myself,
You give a gift of so much wealth.
Go forth my Son into this world,
You're strong, no matter what is hurled.
Irrespective of what I am,
You have become the better man.
As you go on, you'll never know,
Rest assured, I love you so.

Hopeful Dreams and Damaged Nightmares

Queen for a Day

Wearing shirt and tie during the day,
Evening calls, so dress your way.
Make up on, delicately prepared,
Admiration passed, at least you dared.
I know you don't want this distress,
But hey, you look good in a dress.
You passed it off, that it's a trend,
I do not care, I am your friend.
I like you style and your curls,
So very sorry, but I like girls.
Understand, what was intended,
I hope were not, both offended.
It's cool, it's fine, it's all okay,
There's nothing wrong with what you say.
So rock this world with where you're going,
Don't be afraid, just keep on showing.
The greatest ass I've ever seen,
What a drag, this guy, this lovely Queen.

Paul B Morris

Like, Like, Like

Did you see my last post?
So how come you didn't like it?
Were you not entertained?
I thought it was a lovely photo of my dog sat in front of the fireplace doing nothing.
What about my post illustrating what I had for tea last night?
You didn't like that either.
Okay, so it wasn't the best of photos, but it clearly represented the home made spaghetti bolognese.
Why weren't you impressed?
I've liked your posts in the past! Why don't you reciprocate?
Please like my posts.
I'm waiting and still nothing.
What's wrong with you?
I've posted yet another gorgeous selfie, set against a non-descript background.
Why hasn't anyone liked it yet? Why haven't you?
Hey, where have you gone?
You've unfriended me? NO.

Hopeful Dreams and Damaged Nightmares

Princess (Leia) in a Box

My heart was full of joy when I found you,
A treasured piece in my collection.
Your burgundy dress was stunning,
So you were kept in the box for protection.
However, when I looked at you, it lead to disappointment,
They could not get your hair right.
You were nowhere near as beautiful as you were in reality,
It never did you justice.
But, I kept you in the box anyway,
Until the time came when I gave you away.

Paul B Morris

Dark Love

Another day has passed and I'm still not here,
You've taken it all, but left the fear.
Infected soul and murdered heart,
Destroyed a life, torn worlds apart.
I do not live, now all is grey,
These fragile bones, they do decay.
Tattered dreams that burn my eyes,
Nothing left but fractured lies.
A cut so deep that bleeds away,
Surprised I lasted another day.
I took it in, all that you could give,
Despite the hell, I tried to live.
You played it well, with all that seemed,
To tell untruth and curse what I dreamed.
You took my hope and burned it whole,
Left me with a blackened hole.
No alternative than the desire to die,
But I didn't fade, I wonder why?
You cursed and played my tortured mind,
Subjected me to abuse unkind.
Battered me with all your might,
I didn't have the will to fight.
You took a chance, it was your best,
To slash me hard across my chest.
As I fell and began to cry,
You couldn't care if I should die.
With pain and blood, I fell to the floor,
Slowly, did your emotions pour.
You'd thought it through and you were thrilled,
Observing life potentially killed.
As I lay still, silently bleeding,

Hopeful Dreams and Damaged Nightmares

You reconciled a life still needing.
Thankfully I saw another day,
But I didn't live in the same way.
It's irrelevant, you killed me and that is real,
This dark love that I didn't feel.

Traffic

Vehicles trundle wearily along the 2.5 mile stretch of road.
10 miles an hour is the fastest they move, if lucky.
Frustration starts to build as we sit waiting for what seems like hours.
This journey is only supposed to take 10 minutes.
There isn't any obvious reason for delay.
An impatient driver attempts to cut across the traffic from right to left.
Fool. You can't go anywhere. Now you've fucking blocked the road and we cannot pass.
Rage from fellow drivers can be heard several cars back.
Tension in my head increases. I'm going to be late for work. It shouldn't take this long to reach this point.
Driver blocking the road moves on, oblivious to the abuse being hurled at him.

Movement forward lasts for no more than a minute before we grind to a halt again.
At that point, my engine stalls and it struggles to start.
I roar in anger, banging my hands against the steering wheel.
How I hate this morning journey.
How I hate this traffic.

Reflection

Have you ever looked into a mirror,
Not liking what you have seen?
Do you see the reality of now,
Then wish you were in a dream?
Everything is an illusion,
Depicting that you live in greed.
It's just an image of what could be,
Nothing that you really need.
I could show you something simple,
Free from lies they try to tell.
But you've entered into their world,
Buying all they have to sell.
Please will you walk with me,
In the garden of the now.
Learn to enjoy new colours,
Try to forget that life somehow.
Next time you look in the mirror,
Wont you now accept what's true.
As you look at your reflection,
Be content that it's really you.

Paul B Morris

I am Here

You can talk to me.
I will listen.
So, maybe I don't understand this.
Doesn't mean that I don't get it.
I am here.
Always will be.
Should you wish to share with me.
Then do so.
While I may not have the answers,
Or offer anything of relevance,
I can relate.
Even if I don't articulate.
Talk to me.
I am here.

Hopeful Dreams and Damaged Nightmares

Me

Find me.

See me.

Like me.

Love me.

Use me.

Inject me.

Infect me.

Abuse me.

Discard me.

Hate me.

Chaos

Chaos.

It lives in my world.

A frequent visitor.

I wish it would know the boundaries.

I do not welcome it.

Shouldn't be here.

Please accept the territory.

Your place in this life.

Go, I do not need you.

GO.

Who You Really Are

Can't live with you now cause you're full of shit.
I gave you a heart but there's no blood flowing through it.
You had to exist so that you could take all of the blame.
But I made you too real and even gave you a name.
Now you're alive, no longer confined to my head.
Consuming my spirit, wont rest until I'm dead.
You're only happy when I'm completely under your spell.
Breaking me hard and pulling me down into your hell.
But take a good look, stare deeply into my eyes.
See the one whose grown and no longer listens to your lies.

Paul B Morris

Finally

Now that I've decided not to stay,
I can't escape your love that flows my way.
All of life's decisions are now played,
Help me choose the ones that I've not made.
How do I survive throughout this plight?
Show me please, this world that's nearly right.
I can truly feel the love you give,
Now finally, there's a reason to live.

Dark Side Up

With your dark side up,
Your dark side down.
I wanna see how much you're gonna play,
It's been a while and I know you've had a long day.
The camera flashes and now you're in the zone,
You are so focused and you're keeping it your own.
So will you wear a mask?
Guess it's not too hard to ask.
You know it's easy, for me not to be a part,
We really want you to completely enjoy the art.
Sharing the images that flow within your mind,
Tastefully done and expressed with kind.
It's shot in darkness and it's taken right,
Clearly the best image of the night.
With your dark side up,
Your dark side down.

Paul B Morris

The Beautiful Game

Years ago, I loved football,
I played the game when I was small.
With skillful players on the TV,
They used to really inspire me.
But now I don't feel the same,
No longer love the beautiful game.
With so much money on players spent,
Appears to have removed the purpose meant.
Irrelevant of what they can learn,
Players only want to earn.
Indulging in celebrity life,
Expensive cars and a trophy wife.
It matters not how well they've played,
They happily count the thousands paid.
Fans still argue and cause a fight,
Despite the fact the result was right.
This mentality I don't want to know,
Another game, I'll never go.

Hopeful Dreams and Damaged Nightmares

Numb

The beast is closer to me than I thought.
It is real and not just confined to my nightmares.
It lurks within my realm of reality,
Operating within its own duality,
The dichotomy between us is significant.
I have little or no words to comprehend the magnitude of its sinfulness.
I am saturated and infected by it,
Unclean and soiled by its presence
It makes me feel numb.
My trust and my heart are now tainted again,
Bruised and scarred once more.
I breathe in the air that you did and now it makes me choke.
Blacker than tar, it sticks in my throat making me wretch.
I want this reality, this existence not be.
But it is and I can do nothing but accept it.
These familiar surroundings are now stained.
They offer nothing but to serve as a reminder of the beast.
This space is now dead to me.
Yet another emotion is tortured, infected, destroyed and I feel numb.
No longer can I attach any sense of joy or happiness to this place.
Now it is simply a reminder of darkness, pain and suffering.
Thanks for this memory.
My pain is real and it exists,

Paul B Morris

Spilling through in to my world of happiness,
clouding and infecting it too.
The true and real manifestation now penetrating my mind,
Yet another collected demon to lurk within my already crowded nightmares.
I feel numb.

Slave State

Slave bows, he really knows what to do.
Slave screams,
It's less about him and more about you.
Slave dreams,
You have to show him a life so obscure.
Slave lives,
He's happy now because life is so pure.

Please open your mind,
See what can be,
Look outside of so called purity,
Everything is real,
It's just not what you see,
All of this world that lives in slavery.

Slave cries,
She's made a really bad decision.
Slave bleeds,
You have to make a deep incision.
Slave needs,
This is a life she wants to forget.
Slave hopes,
That when she wakes life is not set.

Please open your mind,
See what can be,
Look outside of so called purity,
Everything is real,
It's just not what you see,
All of this world that lives in slavery.

Paul B Morris

Headache

My mind aches,
Dismiss all of these fakes,
But it's slowly ratified.
Too much thinking,
Over analysing,
Yet I operate with pride.
Seeing the colour grey,
Flowing day by day,
Am I truly sanctified?
Being this nothing,
Whilst clearly something,
Paradox is justified.
I still cannot see,
Why you believe in me,
Living so terrified.

Black Waters

I feel like I am falling into an abyss,
drowning in the pool of nothingness.
The water is deep and black in colour,
it is so cold it could freeze on first sight and it
attacks the nerve endings.
Nulling out my senses until I can feel
nothing more than misery,
how I wish it could end.
I would give my life to feel the sweet calm of the
hereafter.
Peering above the murky waters, I see the
reflections of the now,
that's when I see her.
She smiles so warmly, yet it's tinged with a
sadness,
trapped in this world of the damned,
Where nightmares of the past and present
collide viciously.
How she deserves the calm and tranquility of rest.
Freedom in this world of chaos,
freedom from the intoxication that flows through
her veins,
freedom from me.

Paul B Morris

Medication

Another pill,
Prescribed to make me better,
If only that were true.
Every time I consume,
I fall further away,
From the me you know.
Tedium resumes,
Whilst I am paralysed,
Failing to recognise you.
If I was truly free,
I wouldn't be so scared,
Not so easy to walk away.
I am still here now,
Afraid of what's to come,
Surely it's safe to forget a dose?
I do not want to be here,
For you to see me frail,
Please, please let me go.
I know that you wont,
Really love you for that,
But I am losing faith.
What is the point,
Of memories removed,
This pill is a curse.
Drained of vitality,
Grasping humility,
Failed in reality.
Doctors little miracle,
Sticks firm in my throat,
Doesn't help in any way.
It's not worth the concern.

Hopeful Dreams and Damaged Nightmares

Town Guy

Walking through this familiar town,
I meet a man who draws a frown.
It's evident his life's been tough,
He's spent some time living rough.
Face so pale and clothes in dirt,
Eyes that speak of years of hurt.
Offering the coins that I can give,
Knowing it's not enough for him to live.
I cannot know how it must feel,
Struggling to find your latest meal.
No warmth of kind or roof above,
Devoid of friends or any love.
His world is empty, cold and grey,
I wonder if this is his every day.
Offering a smile he shakes my hand,
This gesture truly hasn't been planned.
I bid him well and make on my way,
Unknown if he'll survive another day.

Storm

Storm breaks

Raised stakes

Life takes

Heart aches.

Broken

My heart is now broken,
Because of words spoken.
They were a complete fake,
An ill-conceived stupid mistake.
Words that weren't from the heart,
I beg that we don't fall apart.
Cannot undo what was said,
This lingers deep inside my head.
I'll do whatever that I can,
Please know I'm a foolish man.
In defence I tend to dare,
Sharing emotions because I care.
I hate it when you shed a tear,
Even more when you're not near.
I am so alone when I'm not with you,
Please never doubt my love so true.

Paul B Morris

Down

My thinking, is blinkered, my head begins to hurt,
So useless, and worthless, I'm buried in the dirt.
I'm prostrate, before you, falling to my knees,
Submissive, dismissive, help me wont you please?
So sorry, I worry, that this will drag you down,
Feel guilty, please be free, why don't you let me drown.
You're talking, keep going, it really is so kind,
Something, yet nothing, so I can free my mind.
These tired views, of past life, they slowly turn to hate,
I should ignore them, dissolve them, so they don't seal my fate.
I'm hating, this mirror, because it distorts my eyes,
Keeps showing, me nothing, other than a life of lies.
The darkness, this greyness, it occupies my mind,
Without you, to love me, I'm feeling lost and blind.

Hopeful Dreams and Damaged Nightmares

Crying Clown

Feeling this insecurity, living a life of impurity.
Why do the monsters speak, taking hold of a mind so weak.
Remembering a happy day, one when I didn't feel this way.
Those days when I was so blind, false entries in my mind.
Even now, the world keeps turning.
Yet I fall, so slowly burning.
In my head, these thoughts are keeping.
Degenerating to silent weeping.
I cannot find this happy place.
Or wear a smile upon my face.
It would be easy to simply drown
But here I am, the Crying Clown.
Do I feel the need to die? would it make you cry?
Cannot face another suicide, not a choice that I'll decide.
Irrelevant of what I say, please don't ask me to bow or pray.
It's gone now, so much is black, please don't worry, I'm coming back.
Even now, the world keeps turning.
Yet I fall, so slowly burning.
In my head, these thoughts are keeping.
Degenerating to silent weeping.
I cannot find this happy place.
Or wear a smile upon my face.
It would be easy to simply drown.
But here I am, the Crying Clown.

Paul B Morris

All my Heart

I do not know what I would do,
If I lived in a world without you.
You are my whole life,
Honoured that you are my wife.
I don't underestimate what you give,
Take it all because it lets me live.
You are an angel sent from up above,
Every day we share our world in love.
When I fall you make a stand,
I'm comforted by your fair hand.
All is real when we kiss,
Descend into a world of bliss.
Delighted that our love does grow,
I love you more than you will know.
Accepting that we cannot be apart,
Hope you know I love you with all my heart.

Vitamin D

Ah there you are. Where have you been?
Hiding away like that, is so terribly mean.
I'm saddened by your frequent exile,
But when in your presence I raise a smile.
Brightly beaming warmth upon me,
A natural healthy dose of Vitamin D.
Life seems better and much more fun,
When basking in this sporadic sun.

Paul B Morris

This Life, This Hell

Tired of living in this world I know so well,
Allowing myself to be taken into hell.
Too long have I suffered from all that pains,
Longing to feel the sting of hooks and chains.
Sure that many would find your world with fright,
But I am ready and offer you my flesh to bite.
Devoid of all emotion, I no longer look within,
Dreaming perversely of when you tear at my skin.
Torture and suffering, please try to make me whole,
Readily converted, I willingly give you my soul.
Irrelevantly hearing warnings like I should,
Still, I desire for you to taste my blood.
Hurt me, tease me and then make my naked flesh burn,
Allow my sacrifice to be a lesson for all to learn.

Smoke

I used to smoke for many years,
Now I've stopped to alleviate fears.
Yeah, at first quitting was hard,
But now my lungs don't feel so charred.
No longer do I need to catch breath,
I have prolonged life before my death.
All around me no longer choke,
As they don't consume second hand smoke.
It's now cool that my clothes don't smell,
Got more money in the bank as well.
There's no chance that I will go back,
Realised fears of heart attack.
I'm enjoying being healthy,
Not to mention more wealthy.
Learned that smoke did attack my brain,
I concur because I've felt the strain.
I'll never be a hypocrite,
But I've gotta say, I've never felt so fit.

Offend

What happens if I offend,
With my words that do descend.
Perched seductively upon my lips,
Feeling the tension as it grips.
As I say something wrong,
Because it wont be long,
Before I'm judged or slayed,
By the self righteous or the dismayed.
What was it that I said?
Merely some words formed in my head,
Verbalised and made real,
Not necessarily what I feel.

Words are Alive

I like to play with words,
Shaping them into something colourful,
Letting them come alive,
Allowing them to exist.

Words of love and words of hope,
Or even words that express pain,
Swirl around us as if they were the air,
Seducing us with their magic and mystery.

New words I have learnt,
Excite my imagination,
Helping me to feel alive,
Allowing me to exist.

Paul B Morris

The Brutal Reality of Existence

I struggle to understand,
The mind-set of terror,
Not the type confined to books,
Where we are disturbed by a writer's twisted imagination.

I'm scared by life,
The actions of men and women that unfold,
Causing pain and suffering to the innocent,
Forcing families and friends to grieve.

Who is this devil that guides us along this path?
One of depravity, hatred and evil,
Where life is nothing more than a commodity,
Discarded so quickly through a misguided belief or opinion.

We survive the brutal reality of existence,
Thankfully fueled by our insistence to remain,
Without knowing what comes forth,
Unified as one in the hope that we will live on.

My heart goes out to all the poor souls who suffered in London on this day, Wednesday 23rd March 2017. May you all find peace.

16 Years

It's still the same,
My heart is in pain.
It doesn't change,
I can't rearrange.
What I feel,
Because it is real.
I'm left with fears,
It's been 16 years.
Since you did die,
Yes I still cry.
No we're not apart,
You're locked in my heart.

Silent Voice

Sometimes I curse this world.
I don't understand it's purpose.
Why we're intent on hurting each other?
Or how we allow suffering to exist.

Children die at our hands,
While we debate the right to help them.
Failing to listen to their concerns,
We proceed blindly with our own agenda.

This world is wounded.
It limbers along in pain daring not to choke.
It fears that it is unwell,
Yet is defiant that it will not pass away.

We must do whatever we can,
To make this world more desirable for our children.
Help make it healthy, so they can breathe easier.
We cannot fail our children or this world.

So, where do I fit in?
Where can my voice be heard and not simply ignored?
Am I strong enough to be heard aloud and so publicly?
No, I guess not. Afraid as always, I remain the silent voice.

Something True

Your words burn me inside,
Because you don't speak for me,
Your speech is delivered deliberately,
Without thought causing us to divide.

But why should you care?
You've got propaganda to promote,
Needing the people to cast a vote,
Whilst we're submerged in despair.

The confused are easy to find,
They don't know which way to go,
Too entertained by your show,
Marking the cross and following the blind.

As more and more believe in you,
Succumbing to your charm,
Ignoring what's done to harm,
Please will you offer something true.

Paul B Morris

Legs

They're just legs.
Two pairs of them in fact.
Why is this relevant?
A pointless story to distract.

I just don't get it.
What is the point you're making?
Irrelevant front page news,
Hardly worthy of a story breaking.

Analysed deeper,
It reeks of sexist discrimination,
Nothing relevant or worthy,
Used to sell shite to the nation.

A pointless effort.
Damaging to women everywhere,
Simply wanting to sell and earn,
Ignoring sisters, you don't bloody care.

Inspired by the Daily Fail front page article by Sarah Vine – 28.03.17.

Still A Freak

Monsters didn't live underneath my bed,
They always resided within my head.
A child who removed the heads from toys,
To horrify the other girls and boys.
Would take a graze that hurt so good,
Loved the taste of my own blood.
Not that I considered myself unique,
Just another lonely but pretty freak.
Dressed in clothes of grey and black,
Happy to bring the old days back.
Indulging in the stranger things,
Like helping fairies to find their wings.
You made me out to be a liar,
When you set your doll on fire.
No longer a trend because my life's not so bleak,
But deep down inside, I'm still a freak.

Paul B Morris

Blood

Watching blood spilled,
Causes us to be thrilled.
But not when it's real,
How would you feel?
When it flows from a cut,
Struck by a knife in your gut.
Following a senseless fight,
In the darkness of night.
When you walk home alone,
Via a strange place unknown.
Selecting victims at will,
They're out for the kill.

Hopeful Dreams and Damaged Nightmares

Smile

Walking past you, I smile.
Why do you run a mile?
What did I do wrong?
Did I offend you somehow?

Relax, it's not a signal of intent,
Nothing more than goodwill meant,
Just trying to be civil,
Can you recall when that was cool?

I'm just being polite,
There was a time when that was right,
Now, we have to walk on by.
Portraits of ignorance so very rude.

Please, just once in a while,
Pass by someone and smile.
I'm sure that it really won't hurt,
Might even make you feel good inside.

Paul B Morris

Face

Weird and strange face,
In my head, it looks out of place,
Awkward and disjointed,
With a nose that's too pointed.

Thanks for words so kind,
It's not what I see in my mind,
Not that I care about rejection,
Just really don't like my reflection.

Happy to hide behind a mask,
Wont reveal so please don't ask,
The hate, it builds up deep inside,
Irrelevant, what you now decide.

Yet still I cling to what is true,
You see me and I see you,
Make up covers the scars we hold,
Reading a face and stories told.

Breaking the mask with a smile,
Yes, it happens once in a while,
I look at you and do not judge,
You've not noticed the eyeliner smudge.

Feelings strong, it is a disgrace,
Judging another based on their face,
Too many souls hide within,
They should be free in their own skin.

Alone

Sometimes I feel so alone
Confined to this internal prison
Where nothing inspires or excites me
Forcing me to operate like a drone.

Words of comfort are a waste
They fall on deaf ears
As I close my mind to the world
Not wanting to open up in haste.

Old scars still indicate what's not well
I drown in the sulphur of lies
Cannot recognise the air so pure
Detached from reality and alone in my hell.

Dreaming that someone will save me
As I crumble to the floor
Consumed by demons of life that's past
Hoping that you will set me free.

Paul B Morris

Fake

Fake hair
Fake smile
Fake clothes
Fake money
Fake friends
Fake love
Fake dreams
Fake life.

Knife

Chopping through the vegetables,

My knife it moves too fast,

Slicing through my finger,

I need more than an Elastoplast

This is the Past

Swirling through the blackness of night,
Demonic figures control my mind as the body lies dormant.
I am very much alive but no longer in the world I know,
Yet I recognise the surroundings of the environment I'm now in.
It is a hell most personal to me,
Crafted by intentions most cruel and the beasts are relentless in their pursuit.
Nothing but images of pain and suffering now occupy my thoughts with no sign of release.
I am trapped, merely a slave to these wicked creatures who taunt me without mercy.
Why won't they desist and let me be?
It is constant and it feels so real.
I know that you are near me, but I am so far away and you are not here.
I am lost in the ether of what once was.
It is the nothingness of life, this is the past.
Yet it seems acutely real, painful to the last.
Tormented by the echoes of what was once before,
I arrive back in the now, weak and pained, wanting it to end.

Hopeful Dreams and Damaged Nightmares

Chain Reaction

It starts so innocently,
Before tumbling downward into chaos.
One word or action,
Delivers an image to blacken my suffocated mind.

Unleashed and free,
This disjointed fragment of recollection splinters onward.
It doesn't care what pain it causes,
Selfishly only desiring to invoke pain.

Self worth and positivity are absent,
Drowned in the pool of my own resentment.
The lifeless bodies float in the grey water,
Consumed in the hate of what went before.

Gone but not forgotten,
I yearn to feel the touch of hope once more.
But it is quickly falling further from my grasp,
Leaving me trapped and alone in this world of the never.

It was just one word,
Prompting a chain reaction of suffering.
I am lost in a world so grey and pained,
Will you ever hear my screams?

Paul B Morris

Pain

With sinews strained,
tired muscles crying out,
they move onward through sufferance,
yet desperate for a moments rest.

Respite is not forthcoming though,
duty must be fulfilled,
existing through a struggle daily,
they succumb to failure.

Resignation is obvious,
understood is their plight,
surrendering to the inevitable,
they give in without fight.

Pain does dominate,
causing its master to fall,
crumpled as if in womb,
meekly calling for assistance.

This weakened body cries,
screaming through limbs to mind,
forcing discomfort throughout,
wishing for a sense of peace.

Calm arrives temporarily,
tricking the master in mind,
deceiving into false conclusions,
allowing pain to wait patiently once more.

Hopeful Dreams and Damaged Nightmares

Ink

Discard your technology,
Reach forth for the page,
Read what is written with ink,
Allowing the spirits to roam freely.

Do not hide your passion,
Let free your desire,
Release the books in your care,
For the words are alive.

They will shape you,
Bind and mould you,
Correct or define you,
Inspire and excite you.

Hidden, are so many vessels of words,
Confined to darkness and nausea,
Freed only by lovers such as we,
A prayer for the vendors who set them free.

Dedicated to and performed at, Southcart Books, Walsall, UK as part of the Independent Bookshop Week celebration held on 1st July 2017

Paul B Morris

Dance

Please dance as you see fit,
But do not say a word,
Let the rhythm take you somewhere,
For you do not look absurd.

Hypnotise with me your beauty,
Wrapped within your stunning dress,
Your moves are enticing,
Fuelling love that I do profess.

Desire prompts me to accompany you,
As we swirl across the floor,
Despite my movement being stuttered,
Sweetly you ignore my flaw.

With gentle grace I release your hand,
To watch you dance once more,
I celebrate your gentle moves,
Whilst I look at you in awe.

.

Choke

It is my time,
The stage is free and expecting,
My moment is now,
Words so carefully prepared, most respected and known blindly,
Are now gone as my mind goes blank.

Air escapes my lungs,
Forcing me to fight for breath,
I'm lost inside myself,
Fear consumes my form aggressively, vesting me in a fight so brief,
Until I choke, then the moment is gone.

Paul B Morris

In My Arms

I am whole when I am with you,
for your light drowns out the darkness.
forcing my static heart to beat loudly,
I evolve in a love so true.
Pulling my soul free from the past,
you engage me in the present.
keeping a safe grip on my heart,
presenting me with a love so eternal.
Forgive, that I wonder if I'm in a dream,
for a love like this is surely fantasy,
yet, I do know the answer to this line,
as you are here, in my arms.
Saving my battered heart,
you inject life into my veins,
a drug so wildly addictive,
I consume it wholeheartedly.
There is nothing more to consider,
for all is presented to me in form,
you are here and I know it is true,
relishing this love so fine.
Sweet Angel from up above,
know that my heart is truly yours,
let me caress your sweet form,
forevermore, holding you in my arms.

Also features in 'Within Darkness & Light' anthology by nOthing BOOKS.

Mirror Man

I see myself reflected differently,
Not the vision I have inside.
Lines are being drawn across my skin,
Time will not be denied.

Black to grey then white,
Hair beginning to thin,
Despite these slight amendments,
Little has changed from within.

I have no quarrel with time,
Whatever it holds in surprise,
Drawing new ideas from experience,
Seeing clearly through my eyes.

Mirror man be fulfilled,
Knowing your heart is dear.
To the one who keeps it safely,
Forever young when she is near.

Paul B Morris

Tired

I'm tired of work, with the boredom and stress it brings,
Tired of the pointless sales pitches when the home phone rings.
Tired of politics, especially the nonsense that politicians spew,
Incredibly tired of not being able to express my opinion, without some random fellow running me through.
Tired of the insects who attack me outside,
They force me back in doors to cower and hide.
Tired of the voices that roam in my head,
Why can't they disappear, leave me to contemplate my own thoughts instead?
Tired of the sun that burns too bright,
Which leaves me irritable and restless at night.
I'm tired of lunatics that take innocent life,
Who separate families, child, husband and wife.
Tired that my children cannot go out to play in the street,
Because there is too much concern about who they might meet.
I'm tired

Four Letter Word

Care
Give
Grow
Help
Here
Hope
Kind
Kiss
Life
Live
Love
Save
Soul
Wish
What's with your sanity,
Lack of humanity,
Your desire for profanity,
When using a four letter word?

Paul B Morris

When the Medicine Runs Out

I try to stay together and let the good times in,
But it's hard to resist when the greyness is already within.
Tears line a face that's already scarred,
Then nothing can penetrate this heart that's so hard.
Colours from life gradually fade into a negative,
Forcing me to question what it is I have left to give.
Pain is not physical but it's real and exists in my head,
Withdrawing me from reality and thrusting me into a world of fear and dread.
I'm scared that time is failing and will soon disappear,
Irrational thoughts then consume me causing the onset of fear.
It leads me to retreat and hide within a shell,
As the doorway opens and I stare deeply into hell.
Nothing else left to do but make myself so tight and small,
I know you hate to see me collapse and fall.
It's hard for you to witness as I'm compelled to scream and shout,
Sorry you have to see me when the medicine runs out.

Hopeful Dreams and Damaged Nightmares

Torture me Softly

Pain grips my body tightly,
Relentlessly swirling through me with anger,
Causing me to fall to the floor in agony,
Refusing to accept my plight lightly.
It does not abate,
Cursing my every movement wickedly,
It scratches at every muscle and joint,
Leading me to tempt my fate.
For this pain is just too real,
Crippling and torturing me easily,
Sadistically enjoying the torment,
Delighted that agony is all I feel.
Too weak am I to defend,
Against hate that my body does project,
Weakly I fall on broken knees,
Desperate for the suffering to end.

Something Else Instead

I do not fear what I will become,
Though I am scared of walking blind.
Conflicted emotions wrestle daily,
Beating hard on my bruised mind.
It's way too easy to judge,
Those who surrender own life.
But not so easy to understand why,
So many reach for the knife.
Then they cut their arm,
Category self-harm,
No one's raised the alarm,
It's too late, they have calm.
But, where were you?
Discussing the needs,
Whilst the poor soul bleeds,
Yet another statistic is true.
It's a moment that I dread,
When another one is dead,
Punished by the voices in their head,
But everyone speaks of something else instead.

(Also features in 'Within Darkness & Light' anthology by nOthing BOOKS)

Hopeful Dreams and Damaged Nightmares

Tears of a Child

Such a memory I cannot forget, one that burns into the very core of my mind, punishing me frequently and insisting that an everlasting reminder be left.

Weak, feeble and with the greyness of death beckoning me forth into its collective, I was resurrected by the tears of a child who simply wanted, needed me to exist.

The Most Wondrous of all Spirits

Love, tis such a wondrous and yet playful spirit.
So often it is hard to tame, for it is wild and vibrant, free from boundaries and restriction, fleeting and mysterious at times.
Yet it is real.
Thankful am I that my heart has captured its beauty allowing it to freely wash over my soul.
Some speak of its many identities and that it offers itself easily or with false form, that it is not truly real and only exists in a fairy tale.
But, this is not so, for it flows through those who dare to believe in its magic and embrace its gentle life.
It truly exists within those who will care, nurture and support it, ones who will not let it die.
Love, tis The Most Wondrous of all Spirits.

Hopeful Dreams and Damaged Nightmares

This World for Your Own

Oh sweet child of mine,
Take this world for your own,
Fear nothing at all,
Please continue to shine.

So small but not weak,
I will help you grow,
Allow you to learn,
Give the knowledge you seek.

You are free of fear,
Absorb everything you can,
Embracing our hearts,
I will always be near.

Watching over you,
None shall ever pass,
Protected for all eternity,
My love is forever true.

Paul B Morris

The Jealousy of Love

Jealousy
irrational, suspicious
doubting, hurting, obsessing
insecurity, doubt, hope, assurance
protecting, needing, embracing
romantic, devoted
Love

Prayers

I used to say my prayers every night,
Thanking the 'Father' for watching over me.
But that's no longer the case,
Now that I've seen through the hypocrisy.
Scriptures tell us many a lie,
Blinding us that they truly care.
Sufferance is discarded or falsely cured,
Just as long as you commit to prayer.

Watching Over Us

Nothing remains secret anymore, your browser will betray you.
Sharing your thoughts, activities and desires whilst conveniently displaying adverts.
They're specifically tailored to you, in order to meet your needs, do you not feel lucky?
No escaping this corporate lust, we're trapped inside the machine, this much is true.
Believe me not if you wish, dismiss my notions as simple conspiracy fuss.
You've seen it already, adverts presented on your social media, which should formulate some sense of hysteria.
But they don't, because you accept them as the norm, as you unwittingly conform.
Life becomes controlled by advertising, yet you wont accept that they are watching over us.

Curses in Verses

What is it about curses?
That we find so abhorrent to the point of dread, when heard out loud we turn our head.
They're just words that we can formulate into our verses.
I'm tired of the front,
that disapproves of the word, well, you get my meaning, if indeed I was to rhyme.
Though while amusing, I'll not spend hours abusing, words into a curse.
Yet I too am afflicted, because I'm so contradicted by appropriate use in verse.
You may mock me for taking such a liberal stance, by not wanting to cause consternation amongst the literate,
but I just can't bring myself, in full prose, to rhyme a word as a stunt.

Angry Man in a Pub

Dear angry man in the pub,
why were you getting so vexed?
Your behaviour has left me perplexed, because it wasn't just I that was so inappropriate, if indeed I was at all.

See, I was just happy being me, chatting crap with friends, in an environment that I was entitled to do so.
Sure, our prose was adult, and for that I don't feel at fault, because my verbs and nouns were no more offensive than what you hurled at your kids and wife.
Maybe it's you that should get a life?

So what if I dropped a 'F-Bomb' into my conversation,
Surely that's the risk you had to consider when bringing your younglings into the same location?
I was there to drink ale and not simply pale, to your insignificant indoctrination.

Okay, your kids over heard an unsavoury word, that shouldn't be used in an environment of education.
But, I was out with adult friends, in a place that depends on alcohol consumption, not even one that caters for a nursery.

Adverse as you were to my choice of diction and intent as you were to bring about friction, I stand firm with my point, why did you choose this location?
Let me remind you of your choice of vernacular,

your use of words from the gutter were truly spectacular as they were spat at your offspring and wife.
I was truly shocked at the attitude you rocked, as you directed your family where to sit, not be a shit and to 'fucking' behave..

Fly

Slowly I raised my head, stroking a hand across my eye
Wiping stale tears clear from a troubled face, tired of a life so tattered
My gaze at nothing became disrupted, by the anguished plight of a stricken fly
Crashing into the wall before it fell, I wondered if its life mattered.

Tightly I cradled the troubled fly, hoping dearly that it would live
But my attempts to save its form, forced the insect to begin to cry
Guilt engulfed me as it ended on the floor, as it was all that I could give
So, with a heavy heart I ignored it, and helplessly watched it die.

Hopeful Dreams and Damaged Nightmares

A Life Restarted

I cannot call into question, why you love me so,
yet I do, constantly, for reasons that I do not know.
What is it that you see in my smile, or the definition of my profile?
that makes me want to shout out your name from the roof tops, declaring my undying love for you.
I speak these words with honesty, because they are true.
My world is thrown into chaos when we are parted, just because of you, I live a life restarted.
Your love is real and I feel it saturate me completely and I hope that you feel the reciprocation of the gift you present me?
Because of you, I have realised that there is a life re-energised and it is mine.
I keep growing, fuelled by knowing that there is a love that flows through my veins,
with a promise, that I will not fail you.
A child that lives and grows from our unity, is testament to the community, of two shared hearts that evolve.
Whilst I may not always articulate what is sometimes easy to communicate, know that my heart has always been yours.
If you had seen, what my life had been, then maybe you would understand more easily, why you are my Queen.
For my life would be nothing, if our path hadn't been charted, because you have made me live, a life restarted.

Paul B Morris

Good Luck

Empty – why do I feel like it's my fault?
Head's gone – yet I blamed for this shit.
You act – trying to be all fake, loving and concerned.
Though lost – I know the pieces don't fit.

Scarred boy – I try to resist the blame,
Ignored – still you hide your head in the dirt.
Brother – you blindly deny my pain,
Save face – sweet Jesus this burn really hurt.

Day breaks – leading to more agony,
Kill me – I want this shit to end.
Don't try – to pretend that you care,
It's too late – it's something you cannot mend.

Dark dreams – live inside my twisted mind,
Blood flows – yet you still don't give a shit.
Nothing left – yet I still climb up,
Boy needs help – good luck!

Picture of You

I awake once more after being with you inside my dreams,
this reality is so cold and I am missing you.
I have nothing other than routine, plus the emptiness of being alone,
yet I cling to the one hope I have left, that we could make it true.
If it is only you left in this world that can keep me here,
then know I am falling deeper, scared that I do not know what to do.
Discarding the tears by covering my face with an innocent mask,
keeping close the one thing that I have left, a picture of you.

Sprinkles

As a young boy,
I was thrilled by the sprinkles, which cascaded over my ice cream or angel delight.
Little drops of sugary colour that illuminated my dessert and brightened my heart,
which simply melted, forming new shapes of wonderment.
How those days disappeared quickly though.
Discarded and confined to memory, as age took me to new levels of interest that sprinkles simply couldn't entertain.
Nowadays they have become relevant again, a blast from the past as my young son eagerly reaches a hand outwards,
clutching tightly to his ice cream, he stares excitedly as the sprinkles cascade syrupy colours all over his arm.

Hopeful Dreams and Damaged Nightmares

The Man I Used to Be

I'm not the man I used to be, thankfully, because that guy was a tragedy.
Sure, there were those who rated and others who berated, I just simply hated, the man I used to be.
Blinded by false discourse, I showed no remorse as I went about my way.
Discarding emotion with the most casual notion, I viewed life as a game that could be played.
For better or worse, was merely a verse, to placate all that could see, irrespective of the dismay.

Yeah, such a flirt, enticed by a skirt, oblivious to causing hurt.
But as time has passed by, I woke up to the lie, realising that my life had become grey.
Searching my heart, I knew it was better to part, the life that existed and be free.
For now I've been saved and a new road has been paved.
Thankfully, I'm no longer the man I used to be.

Manufactured Teenage Icon

Plucked from obscurity to become the next big thing,
It matters not that you cannot sing.
You've got the 'right' look and relevant style,
We'll define you and tell you when to smile.
Taking advantage of your innocent passion,
Selling your image dressed in the latest fashion.
What will you do for 15 minutes of fame?
It wont be long before we forget your name.

Hopeful Dreams and Damaged Nightmares

Freedom

When you talk of freedom, I wonder, is it the same for you and me?
Whilst I willingly share a verse, I am in fact locked within a curse, that you may not easily see.
Because in my head, are images of dread, that when observed cause many to be unnerved, as they seem more painful than any words read.
Causing questions to be raised, but I am not fazed, as I will answer most clearly, about subjects that affect others most dearly as long as I am heard.
For most often, I have to soften, the words best used to describe how I feel.
Sadly, there are those who don't see it as real.
You see, a mental health affliction is not an addiction, it is something real, a curse you may feel, without a religious diction.
It affects us all, at times, for it is real and knows no colour, or creed, but it has a need to shout.
Can you hear it? Here it comes in rhyme.
It doesn't care,
If you are black or white,
You'll still have to face it all in fight.
Irrespective of ethnicity or creeds, depression will take whatever it needs, to drive you insane, impart what it will in your brain, deflate and then disown you.
We all hurt and we all cry.
We all live and we all die.
When it's not about you and not about me,
We'll all live together happily and we will be free.

Paul B Morris

Wound

It doesn't matter how much you ignore me,
I am inside you and always will be.
Carry on trying to cut me out of your skin,
You wont succeed as I'm the disease within.
With every random incision you bleed,
Then stop because I'm not what you need.
So wrap your new wound tightly,
Before I reappear nightly,
To torment you onward toward the end,
Living daily in a mind that no one will mend.

Hopeful Dreams and Damaged Nightmares

No Matter

I know hell is calling, but I keep on stalling,
Don't want to reside there any time soon.
My pain filled bones, cause heartfelt moans,
I wish you could hear a more pleasant tune.

No matter what I do,
Senses always sting,
No matter what I give to you,
It's still pain that I bring.

Night is falling, yet I'm still crawling,
This is a curse please break the spell.
With feelings going, no way of knowing,
I'm slowly descending into hell.

No matter what is true,
This is what I feel,
So sorry about what I give to you,
This life is now so real.

Paul B Morris

A Collection of Very Short Stories

From these pages onward, follows a collection of my very short stories.

The stories are extensions of the vast majority of my poetry, dark and emotional.

Some may argue that they are not short stories but are micro or flash fiction. I'm not sure if there is any difference other than a word count. Either way, they make sense in my head which is rare.

Hopeful Dreams and Damaged Nightmares

The Pieces Fit

I know I'm awake but I'm not. All I can see and hear when I close my eyes is white noise. Nothing makes sense, none of the pieces fit. Lying prostrate on the bed, I look up to the ceiling, focussing on the small black shape. A crack, a tear or is it simply just a dirty mark? Is it actually there at all? I don't know the answers, but my gaze is transfixed upon it whatever it is. If indeed it is anything. I muse about what it is. I want to, need to understand it. But it's hurting to comprehend it so I just stare, focussing my gaze and not understanding.

Sounds are all around me, swirling, teasing and taunting me. I'm sure I recognise them as sounds, they are audible to me but not legible. What are they? What do they mean? Do they mean anything and do they have relevance? I don't know, I can no longer focus. Nothing is being processed, nothing is coming through. None of the pieces fit. I'm staring frantically around me searching for some sign, some recognition. Everything is familiar yet so obscure. Am I dreaming? I cannot be sure. I pinch myself hard on the chest, really hard. I feel it, the sharpness of the sting. I feel it, the pain and I'm aware of it. That's good, nothing wrong there.

The sounds come flooding through again drowning in my mind as they all fight to be heard, to survive. They scream for attention, violently demanding to be heard. I wrestle with them fighting to impose order, to take control. Then, they submit and are compliant. They all make sense now, everything does. I'm back "online" like a computer that's been rebooted several times after failing to load. But then all goes blank again, and my "programming" crashes and fails once more and I'm gone, staring at the black crack in the ceiling, if it is indeed actually a crack, or anything at all for that matter.

Where is the reason and the logic? Why can't I focus? What is wrong with me? I shake my limbs vigorously and they respond accordingly, albeit surprised and a little concerned at the ferocity of the instruction. This is good, at least they still respect the chain of command. But relief and fear are juxtaposed and they both state their case to be heard. I guess that fear eventually wins the debate and it strikes fast as my breath shortens, chest constricts while my hands grip each other tightly. They all fight equally for justice, for reason and equality. Unable to find any, all goes blank once more. I'm offline, shutdown by the absence of logic.

Back, staring at the black crack in the ceiling. Am I online again? Is it a crack or could it actually be a hole? Is there something behind it? Another meaning, another world perhaps? Why is it here and why is it relevant and why cannot I understand? My constant questioning brings panic as I feel my breath shorten once more and I gasp for air. I'm alone, trapped and scared. Nothing is making sense and nothing is coming through. None of the pieces fit. "Sorry, you're not online no connection available."

Hopeful Dreams and Damaged Nightmares

I'm here, in the bed, my bed, still lying prostrate. I try to get up but move far too quickly. Dizzied by the experience, I slump back down on the bed. Too much too soon perhaps? My gaze reverts back to the crack in the ceiling. Does it have the answers? No, why would it. I speak out , not loudly though. It's audible but is it legible? She hears it though and reaches out to me, her hand gently caresses my chest. I see her. She is beautiful and I love her. This I know. Her wide brown eyes look deeply into my soul, soothing and calming it's mood. I see the love in her eyes and I know it, I feel it. I hear her voice, she speaks to me. The sounds are so tranquil and they resonate throughout my entire being. I
smile at her, caressing her face with my hand. I say nothing. She looks at me puzzled as if waiting too long for an answer to the question asked not so long ago. Surely it wasn't too challenging to comprehend? I'm confused again. I heard her speak, of this I am certain. I felt the sounds from her voice. But nothing has registered, I've no comprehension of it. It's only her expression that confirms what I believe has gone before me. None of the pieces fit.

My heart races once more and it feels as if my chest is being pressed with force. The fear is creeping in, but I try to hold it back, I breathe deeply. There is a sharpness in my brain as if a needle has been inserted into it's very core. The pain makes me close my eyes fast tightly and I try to will it away with every ounce of energy that I have. I reach for her hand and hold it as tightly as I can. I love her, I need her and I'm desperate to feel her close. "I love you so much" is all I can say while the sharpness rages through my mind, colliding with noises, sounds, images vague and new. I want to scream, I want to reach into my mind and scrape away at this disease, this pain that's so real. I WANT IT TO STOP.

I sense the change. A focus, a new mood, a familiar and pleasing sensation. The white noise has gone and the background is now full of colour. "I love you too and always will" is heard from her sweet lips and it filters through every fibre in my body. It blocks the pain inside my mind and makes it retreat into the past, a memory. I readily enjoy the tender loving embrace and I am happy and thankful. Comforted by her love, I fall back on the bed. Lying prostrate, I stare up at the ceiling, where the black crack used to be. Now I know the pieces fit.

Hopeful Dreams and Damaged Nightmares

Interrogation

At last, I sit in front of him and can look directly into his eyes. He seems completely unfazed by the experience, displaying no emotion at all. He sits there motionless and stares right back at me. No matter, I'll let it go, for now. I've waited a long time for this opportunity to 'talk' to him and I'm not going to let it pass me by. He almost destroyed my life and I need to know why, so that I can gain a sense of justice. "I'm going to ask you some questions and I'd appreciate answers. I doubt they're too hard to comprehend, particularly not for someone of your intelligence. I just need answers. Are you okay with that?" I know my tone of voice is demanding and I don't make any excuse for that. It's irrelevant though as he doesn't make any acknowledgement in the slightest. He sits there motionless and stares right back at me.

Undeterred by the lack of response from him, I continue and launch my first question, no messing around. "So what did you do it? You know, why did you need to break and almost kill me?" Nothing. There is no response at all, not even a flicker of emotion and I am frustrated by it. I don't let it show though, I've got to keep cool. He just sits there saying nothing at all. No problem, I'll take my time, I've got plenty of it on my hands right now. "You told too many lies and people got hurt. I got hurt. You broke and almost killed me. Why? What the fuck did I do so wrong that you needed to punish me so much? What did I do to you? Let me understand, let me help you."

Silence. The man doesn't make a solitary sound. He simply stares at me, unflinching from his gaze. I try a different approach, less direct. "I'm doing okay right now though aren't?" Still nothing. "I mean, you haven't completely held me back that much have you? You didn't win in the end, I survived." Again, he continues to stare back at me without offering any reason at all, no defensive argument, nothing. I feel my temper rising.

He sits there, staring. I feel as if his gaze is penetrating me, looking for some opportunity to get inside and infect it like a parasite searching for its next host. He is unmoving, so devoid of all human emotion. How I hate him right now, how I want to punish him, exact my level of retribution. My mood is turning and I'm sensing the level of anger increasing. How can someone be so astute and un-moving?

The softly, softly approach hasn't worked, so I change my game plan, become more direct. "You fucking tried to destroy me by hurting others, by attacking them mentally, waring them down until they turned against me and aggressively attacked me. You wanted to fuck me up. You wanted me to destroy myself or put me into a position where others would do it. Why?" Again there is no response. He just sits there, staring back at me. His gaze doesn't waver, eyes fixing right upon mine, as

Hopeful Dreams and Damaged Nightmares

if searching for some point of entry, seeking to burrow into my soul. He is so cold and unmoving, I wish that I could strike him, hit him so hard that it would inject some sense of feeling, make some connection. But it would be pointless. I wouldn't gain anything from the action, nothing would be achieved.

Talking to this man has proved a futile experience and I'm more angry, disturbed and emotional than I was before the start of the conversation. I've gained nothing, a complete waste of time. He will not crack, he will not speak. Not to me anyway. He continues to sit there motionless, staring directly at me. There is no point wasting my time talking to this man, one who has no interest in engaging with me. He doesn't want to make any remote effort to defend himself, to show any reason or logic. I am lost and confused, almost dizzied from the effects of this one sided conversation. I still don't have any answers and I'm still in the dark.

I'm done, conversation over. I step up from my chair and walk away from the mirror. Maybe one day I'll try again, who knows?

Paul B Morris

The Lady with Red Hair in the White Dress

She currently occupies my dreams and my woken mind, the lady with red hair. Her beautiful brown eyes softly sparkle in the light and I am instantly lost in them. I long to hold her close and press my lips against hers. I open my arms towards her and she accepts my invitation enthusiastically, pressing her body firmly and reassuringly against mine. Holding her tightly but affectionately, I gently kiss the top of her head as she softly caresses the flat of my back. I feel love's powerful energy flow through me as it cascades against the two of us. We are as one and I am truly thankful. Oh how I truly do love this lady with red hair. This angel, this spirit who has brought me back to life, resurrecting the passing of my heart of which I am honoured to say she know owns.

The past dreams I had of the lady with red hair were constant. She was unknown to me then and I longed to find her, the one, my true love and my soulmate. I recall with great excitement the moment we first did meet and how moved I was by her beauty, instantly lost in the soft glow of those beautiful brown eyes, enchanted forevermore. Irrespective of these visions, I still recall the dark times. Those insipid moments of life when she wasn't mine and neither was I hers. A broken soul was I, verging on consumption from chaos. My only respite from the pointlessness of being was seeing her momentarily, the lady with red hair. Engulfed as I was by my own desperate existence, I almost let her fall away from

Hopeful Dreams and Damaged Nightmares

my touch and my undying love. But my heart and my soul would not be still until they had found sanctuary in the bosom of their true keeper, the lady with red hair.

I fought off the demons that plagued me so and found the courage from within to find her again, to touch her soul with my love. To my utmost delight, it was received warmly and reciprocated in kind. Through the adversity represented by the very means of existence, love was discovered and it was able to develop, flourish and stand freely on its own two feet. The lady with red hair was my saviour and unbeknown to me, so too was I hers. Our formative years were strong and steadfast, our love breathing new life into our souls and new meaning into our combined existence. The new union formed a deep bond between our combined offspring, so natural and healthy that it injected a new sense of purpose within us, particularly in my rejected and bruised heart. Nothing became something, something became possibility and possibility became everything.

Time was kind and accepting of the newly formed existence. It assisted, advised and allowed purpose to be explored. With a heart full of love and hope, I still dreamt of the lady with red hair, be it night or day. But I knew that she was there for me, always, as I was for her. Despite the greyness trying to seep through into my mind, the ghosts of the past daring to reclaim some element of what they considered to be theirs, life progressed beautifully with love and compassion. The dream that I had held so steadfastly, hopefully and passionately became a reality.

I eventually stood there in front of the lady with the red hair in the white dress, so passionately committed and in love. Vows were exchanged and lifelong promises made. How I truly loved her so and how I honourably do so now, even more so than that day, if that is actually possible. How I now exist and live free from the pain that once inhabited my soul. How I will always love her deeply, passionately and truthfully. The lady with the red hair in the white dress has made me who I am. She has allowed me to experience a life that I could and did only dream about. It is real, it is pure and I am truly thankful.

Every day I look into her eyes, those soft big brown pools of love and I am lost in them once more. She is my world, my life and my new dreams. She is my future, my hope and my existence. She is the giver of a child, the most miraculous gift in life. Without her I am nothing, with her I am something and I truly do love her with all my heart and soul. This angel, this spirit so pure, this lady with red hair in the white dress.

Hopeful Dreams and Damaged Nightmares

Silence

Silence is golden, or so they say. But it isn't in my opinion. If you listen closely to silence, you can hear so much. Truth and lies are told in tandem, silently passing you by because you either can't hear them or don't listen.

Take the teacher who instructs the students to be silent on entering the classroom. It never is. You can often hear the faint sound of sniggering hidden behind the breathing of thirty plus souls. Mechanical sounds from electronic devices, wind breaking beneath the doors and people outside in the corridors.

Examination halls demand silence. It's explicitly dictated in big red letters on the board presenting the rules. But it's never truly observed. There is always someone who wrestles with a cough, trying desperately to silence it, but ultimately succumbs to a cacophony of noise, spluttering away in the process.

Observing a minutes silence on the on the eleventh of November is possibly the nearest we get. But it's broken by the sound of disrespectful wildlife chattering and the vehicles of transportation that simply cannot wait to reach their destination.

No, you cannot have true silence. You listen too hard, seeking for the comfort of regular noises. It reminds you that you are alive and that you exist in the present. I doubt even ghosts circulate amongst us under a perfect blanket of noiselessness. They speak to each other, I am certain. Communicating secretly, whispering among themselves. You can hear them, if you listen hard enough. Whoever said the dead are truly silent was either incredibly stupid or plain naïve. They are far from silent, they exist within noise, desperately seeking attention and wanting to be heard.

Try sleeping quietly one night in your perfectly insulated bedroom, where no natural noises can be heard. Other than your own breathing, you will hear noises, I guarantee it. You will hear them talk. The ghosts consume the silence, persisting that they will be heard. You cannot even be silent in your own mind. That's no safe haven you naïve fool. The ghosts will inhabit that environment at the earliest opportunity. They will lock into a person's mind, infect their soul and take residency. It's what they crave. Taking your mind is priceless to them. Once inside, the ghosts will always be heard. They will never cease their constant chattering or passing visions directly into your subconscious. They are noise and you hear them constantly. Ghosts, spirits and other entities will taunt you, particularly in your quietest moments, when you desperately want some quiet time to yourself.

Can you ever find silence in life? Perhaps silence will only be prominent in death? But then, after you have passed, you will exist as a ghost and you will invade the silence of those who live. It is constant and it will always be. Silence is golden

Hopeful Dreams and Damaged Nightmares

This Broken Mind

I take a walk under the soft moonlight again, as I have done daily in the hope it will calm my mood. I need to make sense of everything, well, try to at least. It's not easy though. I've struggled for many years so I doubt tonight will be any different. I guess the answers wont arrive at my door as frequently as the junk mail does.

I walk along this lonely road in sufferance, trying desperately to drown out the sounds emitting from this broken mind of mine. I ignore them explicitly, not allowing them to become anything more than what they are, noise. They are joined by visions, grey and twisted. I need to be alone. If nothing else other than to curse my mind, revolt against the plague it bestows upon me and the pain it causes my loved ones to endure. Guilt now consumes me. Yet another emotion I must fight against, another dark cloud to walk under.

Hearing the laughter once more, which continues to mock me, doesn't assist in anyway. With no one in front of me, I turn sharply to see if there is anyone behind in order to determine the source of the laughter. Nobody is there. It's clearly in my head. Why must I be so tormented? Where will I find respite? It must be him. The Grey Faceless Man. Perpetrator of so many moments damned and lost in my life. My nemesis, my curse and my downfall. I anger him greatly, for I will not completely succumb to his power. I will not allow myself to fall to his darkness and be cursed forevermore. I'll not sacrifice my soul to him for it is has already been submitted willingly to another. One who I know will treat it well and keep it safe. But, The Grey Faceless Man is strong and relentless. He wants to hurt me and he always will.

I've tried to seek answers to this conundrum, to try and resolve the problems that blight me, but it has not yet been fruitful. Sure, I've sat down with those who have been regarded as key holders to the world of darkness, but, they have been too lost in their own environments. Too many times have they fallen into the pool of darkness that they've simply swam away. Simple solutions have been rendered. Taken daily and frequently, improvement surely should have been evident? But this has proved to be no more effective than sticking plasters over gaping wounds. It's been pointless and has presented more issues than originally prominent. Twice, with and without, caused a breakdown, succeeding only to propel me further into the downward spiral. The Grey Faceless Man watched from the outside, laughing to himself as I with tears in my eyes, fell singing 'What have I become, my sweetest friend?' It's not worth the concern.

I walk along the grey roads under the darkness of night, continuing my search for calm. The laughter and voices can no longer be heard, but I still feel the presence of The Grey Faceless Man. I want to meet him in person if I could. I'd stare into eyes, if they

Hopeful Dreams and Damaged Nightmares

exist, attempting to discover his weakness in the hope that I could confront and defeat him.

I've not yet seen him face to face so to speak, although on occasions, I believe I have. It's irrelevant though as I know his presence is real. The Grey Faceless Man stands 6 feet tall and although not too dis-similar to my own stature, he is more toned and stronger than me. His hair is blacker than the darkest of nights and he is dressed in a charcoal grey suit that is always immaculate, adorned with a black carnation in the button hole. His face is featureless, at least, that's what I believe. Though I am convinced he has eyes and a mouth of sorts, for he sees me and speaks to me.

I know of his contempt towards me. It has been festering for years now. Despite my best efforts to free myself from his control, I always end up falling to my knees before him. The Grey Faceless Man evidently takes great pleasure in reminding me that he is the master and I am his slave, subservient to him. Betrayal and wrongdoing on my part is always met with strict punishment. On and on it continues. I don't make it easy for him though. My rebellion grows more frequent and strong. The power of The Angel who now guides me is one to be reckoned with and I slowly but surely, feel the energy flow through me. Alas, I am only an apprentice in these matters and I don't feel confidently ready enough to face my quest entirely on my own, without my guardian angel. I will one day though, hopefully. It is certainly a powerful magic that The Angel has taught me and I work daily, learning how to use my new skills and power.

If only The Angel could be with me daily, I would surely make greater strides forward and would be in a healthier position to confront my foe. But I know that this is not possible and is a somewhat selfish desire. The Angel, my angel, has to watch over and protect other souls. Still, the spirit of The Angel is always there with me and I try to draw strength from this. I sense that The Grey Faceless Man fears The Angel. I certainly hope so.

I reach 25 Walker Road, the house that is empty, abandoned and in a poor state of disrepair. I sympathise with it. In my opinion, the house is still an impressive building, with a certain charm and character. For reasons not obvious from the outside, it remains empty, unwanted, unloved. It stands discarded and I feel an immense sadness about that. I can't help but think that all it needs is one more chance. If the right person or people found it and gave it love and attention, it could be restored to its former self.

25 Walker Road would surely be able to provide a family with warmth, security and love. It could protect them, keep them secure and watch them grow. Standing proudly, I have no doubt that it could become part of the family, filling their hearts with joy. Surely all that is required is for someone to understand it, identify it's problems and doing their utmost to rectify them. Love will surely

Hopeful Dreams and Damaged Nightmares

prevail. If only I had the means to be the saviour. In many ways, this house reflects me. Perhaps that's why I always end my walk at the point I reach it. It serves as a reminder that I am being lovingly restored and that I must now head back home to my loved ones, the family that care and help me grow.

Rain starts to fall and so I make my way home, calmed by the process of this journey and the repetition of the insight that I have come to desire. The darkness mixed with the inclement weather clouds my vision and I am more wary of what or who lurks around the corner. However, my mind is now still and my heart is warm with love, excited about returning home. At this point, there is no sign of The Grey Faceless Man.

Happy Anniversary

As always, I'm late. Traffic has been constant, dense and aggressive. In truth, I've not allowed myself enough time. Forever making sure that I've fulfilled this, that and the other. Jenny had released me from my task, telling me that I needed to get going, making sure I wasn't late, again. I duly obliged, and left work, thankful that someone else actually cared. I had to be on time. It was my wedding anniversary after all. George Cooper's report would certainly have to wait until tomorrow. Mind you, it could wait until the middle of next week for all I cared. I was late though, need to get a move on.

I drove aggressively through the traffic while making sure I remained at a legal speed, picking up the route that lead to The Wexborough Hotel. Trust me, it's better than the name suggests. It's where Maggie and I have always enjoyed our anniversary. We got Married 15 years ago on the 11th February, as near to Valentine's Day as we could arrange and held the wedding reception there. Maggie adores the Wexborough. The décor, service, ambience and most of all, the garden area at the rear. Years ago, Maggie encouraged me rather robustly, to pay for a tree to be planted in this particular garden. It was a romantic idea I guess and a silver birch, whilst initially not much to look at, was planted for her. I'd been informed that it would be quite adaptable in varied UK weather conditions and would most likely outlive us both.

Hopeful Dreams and Damaged Nightmares

Maggie's tree has grown strongly over the years and now stands tall and proud. At Christmas, it looks quite beautiful, elegantly bearing the decorations of the festive period. It stands with prominence and yet with a quiet solemnity as to not cause too much consternation. Its beauty is obvious and yet it doesn't scream for attention, choosing to happily blend in to its surroundings. In many ways, so very much like Maggie.

I just about arrive in time, thankful that there are plenty of spaces left to park my car. Moving with excited haste, I make my way into the Wexborough via the main entrance and head to the bar. It isn't too busy at the moment given that it's the beginning of the typical lunch time period. I'm greeted quickly by a pleasant young guy behind the bar who takes my order for one pint of the latest locally brewed ale, such is my way. I forget what it was called. Maggie doesn't take a drink at lunchtime, so my business is concluded quickly. This appears to cause some annoyance to the older gentleman stood to my left, who believes I've pushed in front of him. He communicates this to me via a screwed face full of disdain while gesturing with his arm. He's holding quite a long piece of paper which I presume contains his order. I imagine it would take at least 10 minutes to process it, mine 20 seconds. I nod and smile casually in his direction and wish him a good day as he begins to berate the young guy behind the bar. There's no need for him to be so rude for heavens sake. Two can play at that game I think, but, it's a special day for me so I leave it.

The restaurant area is far busier than the bar indicated and I have to gracefully weave between the unruly children who are running wild. What do they put in the chicken nuggets and chips these days? I make it through to the pavilion area with my pint intact. It's almost deserted as is the garden area. I'm not surprised really given that it's freezing and snowy ice is still evident. We seem to know winter more in February lately. I feel the cold air again as I make it outside, where only the die-hard cigarette smokers dare to tread. They quickly consume their habit with a speed that's surely not satisfying, desperate to return inside to the warmth. I decide to leave my pint on an empty table because it tastes like shit.

It's very quiet in the gardens and I absorb it for a moment. Birds are chattering pleasantly amongst themselves in a nearby tree and the faint sounds of a busy restaurant can be heard in the background. The Wexborough has an impressive garden which is split over two levels. It looks beautiful in the summer, full of vibrant colour and life. Today though, it is a cold and lonely place. Frozen snow provides a light covering of white over most of the bushes, but the evergreen foliage breaks through, proud that it's presently the brightest colour on show. The snowy grass bears evidence of muddied footprints in irregular patterns, suggesting to me that children have enjoyed playing in the wintery conditions. There are remains of a snowman near to the small playground area. Minus the remaining snow, it's very much how it was on our wedding day.

I eagerly head down the twelve steps that lead to the lower garden where there are more plants and trees, most importantly, our tree. It remains immaculately covered by the recent snow, untouched by the feet of small humans. Perhaps their parents considered it too far away from the smoking area to explore and remain in sight? I don't know. Maggie is there, sitting patiently on the bench that is nearest to her tree, which appears to have been covered in a shower of frosted icing. I stare at her for a moment. She looks amazing. Peaceful and beautiful. Her radiant white dress appears to reflect off the snow, casting a soft glow against her amazing body. Sensing my presence, Maggie delicately turns her head in my direction, her face and smile instantly warming me from the cold. Her eyes shine brightly while her long black hair casually rolls over her shoulders with minimal effort. I love her so much.
"You're late again Michael." She says with a gentle purpose, smiling happily as she greets me.
"I'm sorry Maggie. I got here as fast as I could. I think I've done well all things considered." I reply calmly.

I'm always late. Even on my wedding day I was five minutes late because of road works. Maggie has always just accepted my lateness as being part of 'my way'. She just smiles lovingly into my eyes and all was forgiven. That's always been 'her way'.

I'm aware we don't have much time before she has to go, so we just sit beside each other chatting and staring happily at each other, like hopelessly in love teenagers do on a first date. I want to take her passionately in my arms, but I know it's not the time or place. It doesn't matter though, I'm content with enjoying this moment, in front of Maggie's tree on our anniversary.

"The tree still looks great. Don't you think Maggie?"

"Yes darling, it's beautiful. A lasting reminder of our love and happiness. I truly do love you Michael and I always will." She says with soft conviction, making my heart pound fast and loud in the process.

"I love you too Maggie. For all eternity."

We stare into each others eyes until the point of blurred vision, feeling the love unify us, ignoring the black cloud that circles above Maggie's tree.

"I guess time is up my darling?" I enquire, already aware of the answer.

"Yes my love, I'm afraid so. You need to get back to work anyway. I'll see you soon." She replies softly and reassuringly.

"I know darling. I'll see you later Maggie. Happy Anniversary. I love you." I reply passionately.

"I love you too Michael."

Sadness engages me quickly at the thought of leaving her. I've always detested being apart from my one true love, my soulmate. Blackness descends

Hopeful Dreams and Damaged Nightmares

on to the lower garden, swooping and swirling and I am powerless to prevent it. The air becomes thicker and the silence is broken. Faces in the blackness appear as they begin to take more of a shape. Maggie stands unafraid as they swirl around her with menace.
"Go now Michael. It's time." She shouts to me over the noise generated by these unwelcome visitors. I turn toward the steps and wearily begin to make my way, leaving her alone once more. Before I reach the top step, I turn back to face the direction of my wife who is being consumed once more by the blackest of spirits imaginable. They are spinning around her with an inhuman pace, as if to generate a tornado of pain. Tears roll down my cold cheeks as I stand watching, helpless and unable to save my one so precious. The noise is unbearable, but I can still make out her faint voice over it.
"Happy Anniversary Michael. I love you."
She waves at me enthusiastically and then in one flash, she disappears along with the blackness. All is calm and quiet. She is gone.

Despite being in a frenzied emotional daze, I make it back to my car, un-effected by those around me en-route. Sat inside, I cry openly whilst punching the steering wheel with a rage of hatred and pain. I shout angrily which draws uncomfortable looks from nearby patrons. To hell with them. They don't know. Taking deep breaths, I begin to calm myself and regulate my emotions. I take one of the three remaining cigarettes from the crumpled packet and smoke it hard. I know Maggie would disapprove.

When sufficiently at ease, I drive home declining the need to return to work.

Cancer had taken Maggie quickly and brutally. That was five and a half years ago. From the point of diagnosis, Maggie had lasted just six months. Consultants and Doctors could nothing for her. It was too late for her to survive it. Initially she'd only gone to see her local Doctor with back pain. But subsequent tests and scans had lead to conclude the most unimaginable horror and there simply wasn't anything that could be done for her. Maggie took it all in her stride with the bravery she'd been blessed with. Nothing would ever stop her and she wasn't going to let this get in her way. I did my best to stay strong for Maggie and would keep my sad emotions hidden from her, often crying when she was asleep or when I went to work. Jenny, my Secretary, was a supportive figure in my life at the time. She'd lost her Husband to cancer some years before Maggie was diagnosed, so she was able to offer advice and counsel. It's always been appreciated. Maggie made me promise that I would take her to
The Wexborough on our anniversary before she died and that's what I did.

I watched helplessly as the cancerous beast devoured her to the point where she was barely recognisable, so frail and emaciated. Where pain followed the faintest of movements and yet she stayed so very strong. My love for her knew no boundaries and she was still my Princess whom I adored. My eternal love. On the day of our eleventh

Hopeful Dreams and Damaged Nightmares

wedding anniversary, Maggie couldn't take it any more. She knew death was calling for her. I carried her almost weightless frame to the car, aware of the extreme pain she was in and set off to The Wexborough as promised. She survived the journey, just. Every time I glanced over at her, I could see the blackness taking a tighter grip as her life slowly dissolved. She still managed to smile at me and her eyes spoke of so much love. Maggie, my wife, my love, my life. I would not fail her.

We arrived at The Wexborough on time, a very first for me. Carrying my true love tightly in my arms, I managed to get Maggie to our tree in the lower garden. It was lightly dusted in snow and looked like a scene from a Christmas card. Maggie was clearly tired and frail, so I kissed her gently as the sun cast a shadow over us. She gave me the most beautiful of smiles, before whispering 'Happy Anniversary darling.' Then she died in my arms under her tree.

Paul B Morris

Nothing and Something

Rain is falling heavily outside, confirmed by the rapid rhythm being played out against the window. They are the only sounds present in the otherwise silent office I sit in. Despite the angry persistence of the rain now thrashing at the window as if desperate to get inside, the sounds are somewhat soothing, especially when you close your eyes. I move from the desk and make for the window. When presented with the grey imagery through the glass, the sound of the rain takes on a sinister composition. No longer does it feel soothing as it did only moments earlier. Together, the rain and images are dark and the collective anger appears real. However, I dismiss the threat of whatever the intentions may be.

Bored, tired and alone, I sit uncomfortably in my chair trying desperately to avoid shutting my eyes. I feel hungover from the disruption to my sleep last night which was caused by yet more nightmares. I would give anything to be free from the regular torment and crave the ability to rest. Lately, I have been trying to avoid sleep in the hope it will prevent the visions. This isn't a reliable practice though, as evidenced by last night. The results of sleep depravation have presented somewhat worrying consequences. Coffee serves as a minor relief to my current level of fatigue, but I cannot face a third mug given that it's only just turned 9:00am. I need to sleep and feel I could quite easily drift off, however, it would be inappropriate to do so at this moment. I snigger to myself at the irony of the situation.

The miserable grey sky outside accurately reflects the mood of the offices current occupant. Meandering from one side of the office to the other, I feel the numbness of being lost in my own consciousness. Without distraction on offer, my mind begins to wander off unsupervised. It strays into the hidden woodland rather than staying in sight as agreed. Left to its own devices, it begins to betray me. Simultaneously with the increased intensity of the rain, my mind releases images of darkness and pain to be played out as a macabre slideshow. My inner-self must truly despise me as evidenced by the internal monologue of "You're nothing Jacob, you're nothing." being shouted at me repeatedly. More voices can be heard as they join in the chorus of condemnation torturing my mind sadistically. "You fucking loser.", "You're nothing.", "You're worthless Jacob" and their raucous laughter is all I can hear, apart from the thrashing rain and howling wind. They too mock me. Clasping my hands tightly to my head I scream loudly enough to wake the dead. No one will hear me though as I'm certain I'm the only one here. Even if they did hear my painful cries they wouldn't care, no one does.

I get up and stride purposefully across the office. I need to find calm, Perhaps refreshing my face in the bathroom will help? The un-lit corridor leading from the office presents no sign of life and the connected rooms appear un-occupied, although the darkness could conceal a presence easily. Rain continues to smash against the corridor windows almost drowning out the noise in my head.

The bathroom is cold and the silence is broken only by the slow dripping of a tap. Strange how sounds seem to take on a new meaning when you're alone in near silence, how the senses register noises they've so instantly dismissed previously. Soaking my face with cupped hands, I look up from the cracked sink and stare at the person in the mirror. I recognise him, but he isn't me. He is Jacob Wilkes though. His eyes are grey and lifeless, devoid of all emotion. No redeeming qualities in my opinion. Yeah, I agree with the voices, he is nothing. Jacob Wilkes is nothing at all, a fucking pointless waste of space. I scream out loud once more and punch the mirror and Jacob straight in the face. Confused, I wrestle with the thoughts that consume me from within. My fist is still clenched and blood gently emerges from the fresh wound across two of my knuckles. Turning back to the mirror I recoil at the sight of Jacob who is laughing maniacally. His eyes are now missing from his face, the sockets where they once were are evident, blood seeping effortlessly from the open cavities. Jacob laughs loudly and hauntingly as if he's the only one in on the joke. Transfixed upon this vision, I am compelled to watch as Jacob places his bloodied fingers into the holes that once housed his eyes. His fingers grip at the loose skin and he proceeds to tear the flesh slowly and cleanly from his face, revealing bloodied sinew to the chorus of laughter. I resist the urge to vomit but accept the need to run, to get away from this moment and away from Jacob.

Bursting through the bathroom door I head straight for the stairs that lead to the exit. Despite the darkness, which is only fractionally assisted by an emergency light, I can just make out the shadowy outline of what surely must be another person, stood to the left of me. An arm reaches out towards me and startled by this presence, I lose my footing at the first step of the stairs and fall. Despite the downward trajectory being brief, I land hard on the surface, catching my elbow acutely on the final step's protective metal edging. Pain is minimal but blood is instant and regular. Clasping my elbow tightly to stem the blood flow, my brain reconciles momentarily to advise that a dressing is necessary, meaning I should return to the office. Thanks for that input. On hearing the echo of laughter, I look up towards the top of the stairs to where it seems to originate from, but I can see nothing.

Making to my feet cautiously, I feel somewhat dizzied from the effects of what I witnessed in the bathroom, the sight of the apparition combined with the subsequent fall. Tension is rising within me and I hear the laughter inside my head once more, at least I think it's in my head this time, I'm really not sure. I hear the doors at the top of the stairs swing back and forth. No footsteps follow, so I presume that the presence has now retreated.

I decide to continue downwards and make my return to the office in the opposite direction, taking the longer route.
If it was another person, a colleague perhaps at the top of the stairs, then thanks for the fucking help. I'm unnerved by the whole experience in the bathroom and the presence at the top of the stairs. Was it Jacob? No, that's surely not possible, is it? Was he stood behind me in the bathroom? No, that can't be right, even though he was definitely in the mirror. If it wasn't a person what could it have been? I'm open minded to the possibility of ghosts but think it highly unlikely that it was. I dismiss the notion that it was anything other than my bastard of a mind tormenting me further, trying to break me completely. Guess what? You're doing well, but I'm not giving up yet.

Blood is seeping through the fingers on my right hand that are clasped tightly around the wound on my elbow, dripping periodically downwards. Crimson droplets burst outwards like a firework when they connect with the ground. I don't have anything else upon me that would suitably repress the flow of blood. My right hand looks as if it's been sliced wide open given the amount of blood now collected on it. I move my hand away from the elbow to reveal the jagged smile of the wound, that appears to be speaking silently to me. Whilst only a few inches long, it is quite angry and in need of attention. I'm beginning to feel nauseous at the sight of my own blood, mixed with high levels of anxiety

Hopeful Dreams and Damaged Nightmares

resulting from the experiences of the day thus far.
All in all, it's been a pretty shit day.

The rain is constant. As I peer through the windows
in the foyer, all I can see is the bleak greyness.
There is no sunlight as such, it's being forcibly
restrained by the dark cloud hordes which seem
intent on destroying its soul in order that darkness
can reign throughout. The sunlight fights on though,
it doesn't appear to have given up or lost hope. It
believes that it will break through. It knows it will
eventually prevail by defeating the demons that
attack it. I must follow it's example, I must be
strong. I must fight through my darkness and
prevail.

The sound of the rains intensity is amplified
throughout the vast emptiness of the foyer.
Reverbing all around me and drowning out any
frequencies of lesser audio. However, I can still
make out the sound of laughter, albeit faintly and
with no possibility of establishing it's whereabouts.
But it is there, of that much I am certain. I notice
movement of the door situated to the right of me,
suggesting that it has been opened although I can
see nothing to indicate passage through. An acrid
smell almost overpowers my senses. Never before
have I encountered such foulness and I am
bewildered by its origin. I don't have to wonder for
long. As I turn to make my way to the door, I am
confronted by a monstrous beast, the likes of which
must have come from a damnation below hell.

Standing easily in excess of 6 feet, the beast's muscular frame appears to be reptilian. I recoil both physically and mentally, fear and anxiety consuming every fibre of my being. I freeze on the spot, fight or flight instincts have abandoned me. Slowly advancing towards me, the monster emits a shriek of seismic proportions whilst salivating profusely. "You are nothing Jacob, you are no more." The beast's loud, rasping voice instructs.

The monster reaches me and lashes out powerfully with its vast hand, striking me hard across my chest. The impact catapults me several feet backwards and I land painfully against a wall to a chorus of satisfied demonic laughter. Searing pain across my chest is excruciating. A quick glance downward confirms that there are three open wounds spurting blood angrily. The beast strides towards me once more, blood, presumably mine is dripping from three of the claws on its hand. I cannot move and I feel my breathing struggle whilst my consciousness draws weaker. If this is to be my end, then my last vision is of a powerful demon, the colour of night coming in for the kill. Outside lightening cracks, briefly illuminating the sky, revealing the beast to be upon me. "You are the nothing Jacob, you will die in pain" threatens the beast before it laughs, revealing rows of sharpened and jagged teeth. I need to fight back, but it's pointless. This beast is too physically strong, too powerful and I couldn't vest it even without my injuries. I'd need to be a superhero and not an average nothing. I try almost apologetically to make it up on to my feet, but it's

Hopeful Dreams and Damaged Nightmares

too much and I stumble weakly to my knees, much to the amusement of the beast.

I cough painfully, spewing blood in the process, Yeah I'm pretty damn fucked. I stare at the beast who is standing over me, a predator toying with his prey. I begin to laugh ironically, "I'm not Jacob you dumb fuck. Anyway, I'm not afraid to die. So come on, finish me you fucking piece of shit." I laugh whilst coughing up more blood. I wait for the end, for the beast to strike me dead. My head is gone, overdosing on the cocktail of pain, fear, anxiety, insignificance and terror. These final moments are confusing and I've never felt so alone. I don't want this. I don't want to die. But I cannot fight this fear of the inevitable.

"Ha Ha Ha, you are nothing Jacob and you know this. You don't need eyes to see that you are nothing" rasps the beast as it reaches for me. With a final act of defiance, I muster what remains of my strength and swing a clenched fist at the beast. It's a futile and painful exercise for me anyway. The dark beast catches my hand without effort. Pulling it upwards and back against its allowed angle, the beast snaps it virtually in two away from the wrist exposing the bones and tendons from beneath. My pained screams almost drown out the sound of thunderous weather outside and I nearly feel the voluntary need to slip away from this life, unable to take the torture any more. I cannot focus on anything other than the incredible pain I am in, but I don't want to die. My breathing is slow, debilitated from the attack and vision is becoming increasingly blurred. There is no mistaking the beast though as he looms closer, moving in for the kill. "Your soul is mine nothing." crows the beast. "No, my soul belongs to another. It always has and always will. So fuck you." My final words are very eloquently put. I can't comprehend what's actually happening although there is only a little confusion. I saw Jacob rip off his own face and yet the beast calls me by that name. Has the monster mistaken me for Jacob or am I actually him?

An explosion of lightening illuminates the foyer as the rain continues to pelt the windows. The beast reaches out for me and I smile at it. "Die nothing, die." It says as it clasps its clawed hands either side of my head. My time is up and I'm going to die. I stare at the beast silently as it rams it's clawed thumbs into my eyes, forcing them back into the centre of my skull. Then, all is quiet. The pain has gone and all is peaceful.

Startled I awake, covered in sweat and with my heart beating relentlessly. My breathing struggles to regulate itself at first but eventually finds a sense of rhythm as I take in the surroundings. It hits me. I can see. I can actually see. My last recollection was that my eyes were taken from me by the beast. What the fuck is happening? Scared and confused, I make sense of the images before me, confirming that I am in the bedroom that I share with Nicola and I am alone in bed. Familiar sounds of aggressive rainfall can be heard against the windows supported by the bassline of thunder. The storm was or is real, I think? Sweat runs heavily from my brow as I struggle for recollection, attempting to make sense of what is happening. My mind is cloudy and pain shoots from the temples making everything seem grey and jagged. Is this the remnant of, or the introduction to, either a migraine or anxiety attack? I cannot be certain. I rise sharply from underneath the duvet and step out of the bed. My left arm is painful and numb from the sensation of pins and needles, suggesting that I've lay on it awkwardly. Urgently inspecting the elbow, I don't see the mouth-like open wound smiling back at me. "What the fuck?" I mutter blankly. Confusion levels are running ten-fold. I distinctly recall gashing my elbow on the stairs and blood being everywhere, but where and when did this happen?

The door immediately to my right opens quickly and an angel dressed in a flowing white gown walks through it. She instantly recognises my face and makes her way to me. "Jacob my darling, are you ok? You were tossing and turning in bed last night and you looked in so much pain again. Oh baby, my troubled and precious one." Her words are soft like silk and they sooth me. She embraces me tightly, tenderly and I can feel the love. I pull her closer still until she is more or less part of me, greedily kissing her neck. I cry unreservedly in her arms and she allows it, stroking my head gently to encourage the exorcism of emotion. "Nicola, what the fuck is wrong with me?" I ask painfully. "There's nothing wrong with you baby. It's ok, you just had a really terrible nightmare. But it's ok Jacob, I'm here." She tries her best to reassure me and her love is felt wholeheartedly. "Talk to me Jacob, you know that you can. You were so animated in your sleep I was getting scared. I tried to wake you but you were gone so deeply. Did you take your medication before bed?" she questions softly. "I, I, I don't know what was happening and I'm not sure if I did take my meds. Did I? Can't remember. Everything's a blank again and now my head fucking kills." I reply meekly. I'm confused still and my head is spinning with noise, blurred images and pain. I feel ashamed and guilty for upsetting Nicola like this, I don't want her to suffer. She holds me tightly and whispers "I love you" in my ear and she tells me that it's for all eternity and that her soul is mine. How I love her with a passion. The sensation of love, of being alive, being wanted and being something washes through me, cleansing as it goes.

Lightening strikes outside once more, illuminating the bedroom with a pale electric blue colour. Nicola clenches me tightly. My mind seems clearer and provides some order of last nights event. I play them back and I am disturbed by them. I wish I could tell Nicola about the beast and how it sliced open my stomach and removed my eyes. How I seemed to visualise my own death. How I witnessed Jacob, my own reflection, removing my own face. But how the fuck could I tell her any of that? What would she think of me? Surely if she heard this horror story she'd freak out and maybe even leave me? No, the love I feel from her powerful embrace tells me otherwise and I begin talking and relaying the events from last night as I saw them. During the tale, she winces a couple of times and squeezes me tightly. Her eyes fill as she hears the torture that I went through. "I love you Jacob and I always will. You are something. You're a husband, father, lover and my eternal soulmate." Boasts Nicola proudly and I reciprocate in kind. I feel so alive and I really do feel like something.

We start to kiss passionately and fall backwards onto the bed. Nicola is on top of me and I pull her closely, tugging at her clothing to loosen it. The top of her long white gown opens and falls down from her shoulders. She sits upright and begins to pull my t-shirt upwards away from body. She throws my shirt over her shoulder, staring lustfully at my chest. Then she screams loudly and fearfully. She jumps away from me fighting to keep hold of her gown. I jump up in her direction. She cries and points at me, startled and visibly frightened. "What the fuck is that across your stomach? What the fuck is going on Jacob?" She demands hysterically. I look down at my naked torso to inspect, instantly horrified and disturbed by what I've seen. For there are three long, jagged and recently healed scars. They look as if they've been left by something sharp, like a hunting knife or more accurately, claws.

Where Are You?

"Daddy, Daddy. Where are you Daddy?" comes the voice of the young girl once more. I've always heard it speak to me, yet I have no idea from where it originates. The voice is feint, weak and distorted. But I still hear it clearly, as if it were spoken directly to me and it tears at my soul. "Daddy, Daddy. Where are you? Why wont you talk to me? Please talk to me." She pleads, despite my vague efforts, I have no idea how to connect. "I'm here." I shout in the dead of night, but there is no one else around. All is blank and all is silent. There is nothing in this moment other than heartache and pain. I feel it too but have no understanding of why these emotions affect me. I call out again, "Where are you child? Are you suffering? Why do you call me?" but there is only silence, for now.

Closing my eyes tightly, I am engulfed in noise, that whilst incoherent, it is angry. I try hard to focus on other thoughts, ones more recent. But it's not possible and I cannot prevent myself from seeing her there in front of me. The little angel is sat quietly cradling a battered cuddly toy that no longer has eyes or a mouth. Her white dress is now old, tattered and filthy. Her long auburn hair hangs limply over her narrow shoulders matted and lifeless. She plays absently with her toy, rocking slowly backwards and forwards. Her sad brown eyes stare into the distance as she waits patiently for something or someone to appear. She's always

Hopeful Dreams and Damaged Nightmares

waited, calling out into the night, wanting to be heard.

"Daddy, Daddy. Where are you? Why wont you play games with me? Can't we go to the park? Why won't you talk to me?" She pleads once more, her eyes filled with fear as the darkness begins to creep up behind her. I call out to her, but I cannot be heard. Shouting with all my might while banging aggressively on the transparent walls that now suddenly surround me. I can do nothing but watch as the nefarious beings swirl around her. "Get away from her you bastards." I shout in vein, as the beings simply look directly at me and laugh.

"Daddy, Daddy. I'm scared. Please come here and save me. Where are you? Please be with me. I need you." She cries and clutches the battered teddy closer in, needing to draw some comfort from it. None is received as the toy bursts into flames, burning in her hands. She drops it to the floor quickly before it dissolves into thick black acrid smoke. She looks incredibly sad, pained and I wish I could help in some way. I call out to her offering words of comfort, trying to reassure her. But I cannot be heard, it's pointless. The ghosts laugh wickedly, cruelly feeding off the little girl's pain.

Curling up tightly into a little frail ball, the girl's tattered dress slowly turns to a dark shade of charcoal grey. Her face becomes paler and her eyes weigh heavy with sadness. I cannot hear her voice, but she is whimpering softly as the evil spirits gradually consume her face. The girl is dying, I am certain. Shouting out and pummelling the glass walls with rage, I try my damnedest to be heard and to smash my way through to save her. But it is all to no avail and I am helpless to prevent the spirits from mercilessly swirl around her to the sound of their sickening chorus of screams.

She cries, it is weak and feeble, resigned to being constantly ignored. "Daddy, Daddy, where are you? What have I done wrong? Why don't you care? Please, please, help me." Her voice tinged with sadness and resignation, knowing to well that help will not be received. The ghosts circulate around her in greater numbers and at speed until all I can see is a hurricane of blackened evil. It's too late. I cannot reach her. I have failed once more. The little girls muted scream is silenced as she is consumed whole. The spirits evaporate into a black mist twinned with a sharp piercing sound until all is still. She is dead. Gone, without anyone to help or save her in the hour of need. Alone in her final moments of life.

I cry as I have done many times before, but I know my tears lack soul or meaning. Hopeless and useless actions or notions from my part have borne no meaning to the little girl's life. I am lost in the nothingness of my own self-loathing, consumed by the darkness that exists with the grey heart of mine. Just another faded memory correlating to it's appropriate physical scar.

Hopeful Dreams and Damaged Nightmares

I manage to settle my thoughts and in doing so, find some calm and composure. Rested, I begin to drift towards the moment before sleep. There I can hear the faint sound of a little girl calling out hopefully and excitedly "Daddy, Daddy. Where are you?"

Paul B Morris

Paul B Morris is a poet and writer who hails from Walsall in the West Midlands, although he was possibly created somewhere up North.

His stories lean towards dark fiction, horror and the strange, whilst his poetry tends to draw focus from the dark reality of life. He apologises for that.

After falling in love with the work of the great Shakespeare, Morris has also drawn inspiration from Lewis Carroll, Stephen King, Graham Masterton and most notably, Michael Marshall Smith, who is still his favourite author.

In the realms of normality, Paul B Morris is happily married to an Angel, has four children who constantly get the better of him and wishes that he had the time to care for a pet bat. He owns two red t-shirts that don't suit him.

If interested, you can follow Paul B Morris @

https://paulbmorrismedia.wordpress.com/

https://www.facebook.com/paulbmorrisauthor/

https://twitter.com/pbmorriswriter/

Published work

Within Darkness & Light – A Collection of Poetry compiled and edited by Paul B Morris *published by nOthing bOOKS*

Poetry

'Hey Maggie' & 'The Grey Man' – Featured in 'Beautiful Tragedies' *published by HellBound Books*

'Grow Little Ones Grow & This World' – Featured in 'Diverse Verse 2' *published by Walsall Poetry Society*

'I am The Black Mist' – Featured in 'Supersick – Tales of Twisted Superheroes'

Short Horror Stories

'Hail Mary' – Featured in 'The Reverend Burdizzo's Hymn Book' *published by Burdizzo Books*

Thank you for reading this far. Go now, do something more interesting!

Paul B Morris

I
I AM
I AM sOmething
I AM sOmething gOod

nOthing BOOKS

To Elaine

Thank you
for your support

love
Paul B

Made in the USA
Columbia, SC
15 January 2018